From Trash to Treasures

Jars and Pots

Daniel Nunn

Heinemann Library
Chicago, Illinois

www.heinemannraintree.com
Visit our website to find out more information about Heinemann-Raintree books.

To order:
☎ Phone 888-454-2279
🖥 Visit www.heinemannraintree.com to browse our catalog and order online.

Edited by Rebecca Rissman, Daniel Nunn, and Sian Smith
Designed by Joanna Hinton-Malivoire
Picture research by Tracy Cummins
Originated by Capstone Global Library Ltd
Printed in the United States of America in Stevens Point, Wisconsin.

062011
006273

Library of Congress Cataloging-in-Publication Data
Nunn, Daniel.
  Jars and Pots / Daniel Nunn.—1.
     pages cm.—(From Trash to Treasures)
  Includes bibliographical references and index.
  ISBN 978-1-4329-5154-2 (hc)—ISBN 978-1-4329-5163-4 (pb) 1. Handicraft—Juvenile literature. 2. Containers—Juvenile literature. 3. Salvage (Waste, etc.)—Juvenile literature. I. Title.
  TT160.N78 2011
  745.5—dc22   2010049828

Acknowledgments
We would like to thank the following for permission to reproduce photographs: Corbis pp. 9, 23d (© Franz-Peter Tschauner/dpa); Heinemann Raintree pp. 6, 8, 10, 11, 12, 13, 14, 15, 16, 17, 18, 19, 20, 21, 23a, 23f (Karon Dubke), 22c (David Rigg); istockphoto pp. 7 (© Serhiy Zavalnyuk), 23e (© Ian Poole); Shutterstock pp. 4 (© donatas1205), 5, 23b (© Robert Gebbie Photography), 22a (© Andy Piatt), 22b (© grynold), 23c (© donatas1205).

Cover photograph of jars, a pot, and jar animals, and back cover photographs of a bird bath and a wind chime reproduced with permission of Heinemann Raintree (Karon Dubke).

Every effort has been made to contact copyright holders of material reproduced in this book. Any omissions will be rectified in subsequent printings if notice is given to the publisher.

Contents

Some words are shown in bold, **like this**. You can
find them in the glossary on page 23.

What Are Jars and Pots?

A jar is a round **container** with a lid.

Most jars are made of glass.

A pot is a deep container used for storing things, cooking, or for growing plants.

Many pots are **ceramic**.

What Happens When You Throw Jars and Pots Away?

Jars and pots are very useful.

But when you have finished with them, do you throw them away?

If so, then your jars and pots will end up at a garbage dump.

They will be buried in the ground and may stay there for a very long time.

What Is Recycling?

It is much better to **recycle** glass jars than to throw them away.

Separate glass jars from your other trash and put them in a recycling bin.

The glass things will be collected and taken to a **factory**.

Then the glass will be made into something new.

How Can I Reuse Old Jars and Pots?

You can also use old jars and pots to make your own new things.

When you have finished with a jar or pot, put it somewhere safe instead of throwing it away.

Soon you will have lots of jars and pots waiting to be reused.

You are ready to turn your trash into treasures!

What Can I Make with Ceramic Pots?

You can use **ceramic** pots to make a bird bath.

Then birds can use it to wash in and drink water.

You can also use flower pots to make a wind chime.

Hang it anywhere and wait for the wind to blow!

What Can I Make with Glass Jars?

Old glass jars can be made into beautiful snow globes.

Remember to keep and use the lids, or the water will spill out!

You can also use an old jam jar to make an **air freshener**.

This jar has **potpourri** inside to make a room smell nice.

Have you ever seen a toy fish tank in a jar?

It would make a great Father's Day present!

You can also use jars and pots to make your own toys.

These baby animals have been made out of baby food jars and a flower pot.

Make Your Own Trinket Tree

If your bedroom is always messy, maybe you should make a trinket tree.

You will need a flower pot, modeling clay, cotton batting, twigs, and some silver paint.

First, roll a large piece of modeling clay and place it in the flower pot.

Then, fill the pot with cotton batting, so that the modeling clay is hidden.

Next, paint your twigs silver.

You could put them on old newspaper to keep the table clean.

When the paint has dried, push the twigs through the cotton batting and into the modeling clay.

Now you can hang your trinkets on the branches!

Recycling Quiz

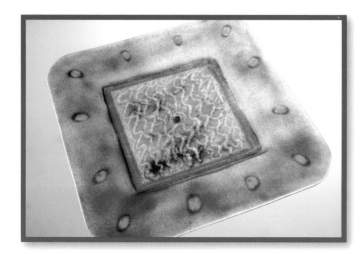

One of these things is made from **recycled** glass. Can you guess which one? (The answer is on page 24.)

Glossary

 **air freshener** something that is used to make a room smell nicer

 **ceramic** clay that has been baked in a very hot oven until it is hard

 **container** object used to put things in

 **factory** building where something is made

 **potpourri** mixture of dried flowers and spices that smells nice

 **recycle** break down a material and use it again to make something new

Find Out More

Ask an adult to help you make fun things with jars and pots using the Websites below.

Bird bath: **www.craftsforkids.com/projects/bird_bath.htm**

Snow globe: **http://pbskids.org/zoom/activities/do/snowglobe.html**

Other ideas can be found at the following website. Click on "jars": **http://www.artistshelpingchildren.org/craftsbyitems.html**

Answer to question on page 22
The square mat is made from recycled glass.

Index